WHY I WAKE EARLY

WHY I WAKE EARLY

NEW POEMS BY

Mary Oliver

BEACON PRESS

BOSTON

Beacon Press
25 Beacon Street
Boston, Massachusetts 02108-2892
www.beacon.org

Beacon Press books
are published under the auspices of
the Unitarian Universalist Association of Congregations.

Text design by Dede Cummings/DCDESIGN

08 07 06 05 04   8 7 6 5 4 3 2 1
ISBN 0-8070-6876-4
This book is printed on acid-free paper that meets the
uncoated paper ANSI/NISO specifications for permanence
as revised in 1992.

Library of Congress Control Number
2004100205

For

Molly Malone Cook

CONTENTS

PART ONE

PART TWO

"Lord! who hath praise enough?"

–George Herbert

WHY I WAKE EARLY

PART
ONE

Why I Wake Early

Hello, sun in my face.
Hello, you who make the morning
and spread it over the fields
and into the faces of the tulips
and the nodding morning glories,
and into the windows of, even, the
miserable and the crotchety—

best preacher that ever was,
dear star, that just happens
to be where you are in the universe
to keep us from ever-darkness,
to ease us with warm touching,
to hold us in the great hands of light—
good morning, good morning, good morning.

Watch, now, how I start the day
in happiness, in kindness.

Bone

Understand, I am always trying to figure out
what the soul is,
and where hidden,
and what shape—

and so, last week,
when I found on the beach
the ear bone
of a pilot whale that may have died

hundreds of years ago, I thought
maybe I was close
to discovering something—
for the ear bone

2.

is the portion that lasts longest
in any of us, man or whale; shaped
like a squat spoon
with a pink scoop where

once, in the lively swimmer's head,
it joined its two sisters
in the house of hearing,
it was only

two inches long—
and I thought: the soul
might be like this—
so hard, so necessary—

3.

yet almost nothing.
Beside me
the gray sea
was opening and shutting its wave-doors,

unfolding over and over
its time-ridiculing roar;
I looked but I couldn't see anything
through its dark-knit glare;

yet don't we all *know*, the golden sand
is there at the bottom,
though our eyes have never seen it,
nor can our hands ever catch it

4.

lest we would sift it down
into fractions, and facts—
certainties—
and what the soul is, also

I believe I will never quite know.
Though I play at the edges of knowing,
truly I know
our part is not knowing,

but looking, and touching, and loving,
which is the way I walked on,
softly,
through the pale-pink morning light.

Freshen the Flowers, She Said

So I put them in the sink, for the cool porcelain
    was tender,
and took out the tattered and cut each stem
    on a slant,
trimmed the black and raggy leaves, and set them all—
    roses, delphiniums, daisies, iris, lilies,
and more whose names I don't know, in bright new water—
    gave them

a bounce upward at the end to let them take
    their own choice of position, the wheels, the spurs,
the little sheds of the buds. It took, to do this,
    perhaps fifteen minutes.
Fifteen minutes of music
    with nothing playing.

Where Does the Temple Begin,
Where Does It End?

There are things you can't reach. But
you can reach out to them, and all day long.

The wind, the bird flying away. The idea of God.

And it can keep you as busy as anything else, and happier.

The snake slides away; the fish jumps, like a little lily,
out of the water and back in; the goldfinches sing
     from the unreachable top of the tree.

I look; morning to night I am never done with looking.

Looking I mean not just standing around, but standing around
     as though with your arms open.

And thinking: maybe something will come, some
     shining coil of wind,
     or a few leaves from any old tree—
          they are all in this too.

And now I will tell you the truth.
Everything in the world
comes.

At least, closer.

And, cordially.

Like the nibbling, tinsel-eyed fish; the unlooping snake.
Like goldfinches, little dolls of gold
fluttering around the corner of the sky

of God, the blue air.

Beans

They're not like peaches or squash. Plumpness isn't for them. They like being lean, as if for the narrow path. The beans themselves sit quietly inside their green pods. Instinctively one picks with care, never tearing down the fine vine, never not noticing their crisp bodies, or feeling their willingness for the pot, for the fire.

I have thought sometimes that something—I can't name it—watches as I walk the rows, accepting the gift of their lives to assist mine.

I know what you think: this is foolishness. They're only vegetables. Even the blossoms with which they begin are small and pale, hardly significant. Our hands, or minds, our feet hold more intelligence. With this I have no quarrel.

But, what about virtue?

The Arrowhead

The arrowhead,
which I found beside the river,
was glittering and pointed.
I picked it up, and said,
"Now, it's mine."
I thought of showing it to friends.
I thought of putting it—such an imposing trinket—
in a little box, on my desk.
Halfway home, past the cut fields,
the old ghost
stood under the hickories.
"I would rather drink the wind," he said,
"I would rather eat mud and die
than steal as you still steal,
than lie as you still lie."

Trout Lilies

It happened I couldn't find in all my books
more than a picture and a few words concerning
the trout lily,

so I shut my eyes.
And let the darkness come in
and roll me back.
The old creek

began to sing in my ears
as it rolled along, like the hair of spring,
and the young girl I used to be
heard it also,

as she came swinging into the woods,
truant from everything as usual
except the clear globe of the day, and its
beautiful details.

Then she stopped,
where the first trout lilies of the year
   had sprung from the ground
with their spotted bodies
and their six-antlered bright faces,
and their many red tongues.

If she spoke to them, I don't remember what she said,
and if they kindly answered, it's a gift that can't be broken
   by giving it away.
All I know is, there was a light that lingered, for hours,
under her eyelids—that made a difference
when she went back to a difficult house, at the end of the day.

The Poet Goes to Indiana

I'll tell you a half-dozen things
that happened to me
in Indiana
when I went that far west to teach.
You tell me if it was worth it.

I lived in the country
with my dog—
part of the bargain of coming.
And there was a pond
with fish from, I think, China.
I felt them sometimes against my feet.
Also, they crept out of the pond, along its edges,
to eat the grass.
I'm not lying.
And I saw coyotes,
two of them, at dawn, running over the seemingly
unenclosed fields.
And once a deer, but a buck, thick-necked, leaped
into the road just—oh, I mean just, in front of my car—
and we both made it home safe.
And once the blacksmith came to care for the four horses,
or the three horses that belonged to the owner of the house,
and I bargained with him, if I could catch the forth,
he, too, would have hooves trimmed
for the Indiana winter,
and apples did it,
and a rope over the neck did it,

so I won something wonderful;
and there was, one morning,
an owl
flying, oh pale angel, into
the hay loft of a barn,
I see it still;
and there was once, oh wonderful,
a new horse in the pasture,
a tall, slim being—a neighbor was keeping him there—
and she put her face against my face,
put her muzzle, her nostrils, soft as violets,
against my mouth and my nose, and breathed me,
to see who I was,
a long quiet minute—minutes—
then she stamped feet and whisked tail
and danced deliciously into the grass away, and came back.
She was saying, so plainly, that I was good, or good enough.
Such a fine time I had teaching in Indiana.

The Snow Cricket

Just beyond the leaves and the white faces
of the lilies,
I saw the wings
of the green snow cricket

as it went flying
from vine to vine,
searching, then finding a shadowed place in which
to sit and sing—

and by singing I mean, in this instance,
not just the work of the little mouth-cave,
but of every enfoldment of the body—
a singing that has no words

or a single bar of music
or anything more, in fact, than one repeated
rippling phrase
built of loneliness

and its consequences: longing
and hope.
Pale and humped,
the snow cricket sat all evening

in a leafy hut, in the honeysuckle.
It was trembling
with the force
of its crying out,

and in truth I couldn't wait to see if another would come to it
for fear that it wouldn't,
and I wouldn't be able to bear it.
I wished it good luck, with all my heart,

and went back over the lawn, to where the lilies were standing
on their calm, cob feet,
each in the ease
of a single, waxy body

breathing contentedly in the chill night air;
and I swear I pitied them, as I looked down
into the theater of their perfect faces—
that frozen, bottomless glare.

The Lover of Earth Cannot Help Herself

In summer,
    through the fields
        of wild mustard,
            then goldenrod,

I walk, brushing
    the wicks
        of their bodies
            and the bright hair

of their heads—
    and in fact
        I lie down
            that the little weightless pieces of gold

may float over me,
    shining in the air,
        falling in my hair,
            touching my face—

ah, sweet-smelling,
    glossy and
        colorful world,
          I say,

even as I begin
    to feel
        my left eye then the right eye
            begin to burn

and twitch
    and grow very large—
      even as I begin
        to weep,

to sneeze
    in this irrepressible
      seizure
        of summerlove.

Have You Seen Blacksnake Swimming?

Down at Blackwater
blacksnake went swimming, scrolling
close to the shore, only
his head above the water, the long
yard of his body just beneath the surface,
quick and gleaming. The day was hot, but there
in the water, another snake might have
danced with him. But, since he was alone
he whirled a little, unnecessarily, and picked up speed,
so that on both sides he made a lacy wake
and there was a rippling sound,
a sort of soft music, just enough
to amuse that narrow mouth, whose corners,
in that coolness, were lifted in even more
than his usual gentleman's smile.

How Everything Adores Being Alive

What
   if you were
      a beetle,
         and a soft wind

and a certain allowance of time
   had summoned you
      out of your wrappings,
        and there you were,

so many legs
   hardening,
      maybe even
        more than one pair of eyes

and the whole world
   in front of you?
      And what if you had wings
        and flew

into the garden,
   then fell
      into the up-tipped
        face

of a white flower,
   and what if you had
      a sort of mouth,
        a lip

to place close
   to the skim
      of honey
         that kept offering itself—

what would you think then
   of the world
      as, night and day,
         you were kept there—

oh happy prisoner—
   sighing, humming,
      roaming
         that deep cup?

Clouds

All afternoon, Sir,
your ambassadors have been turning
into lakes and rivers.
At first they were just clouds, like any other.
Then they swelled and swirled; then they hung very still;
then they broke open. This is, I suppose,
just one of the common miracles,
a transformation, not a vision,
not an answer, not a proof, but I put it
there, close against my heart, where the need is, and it serves

the purpose. I go on, soaked through, my hair
slicked back;
like corn, or wheat, shining and useful.

Spring at Blackwater: I Go Through the Lessons Already Learned

He gave the fish
her coat of foil,
and her soft eggs.
He made the kingfisher's
quick eye
and her peerless, terrible beak.
He made the circles
of the days and the seasons
to close tightly,
and forever—

then open again.

The Lily

Night after night
   darkness
      enters the face
      of the lily

which, lightly,
   closes its five walls
      around itself,
        and its purse

of honey,
   and its fragrance,
      and is content
        to stand there

in the garden,
   not quite sleeping,
      and, maybe,
        saying in lily language

some small words
   we can't hear
      even when there is no wind
        anywhere,

its lips
   are so secret,
      its tongue
        is so hidden—

or, maybe,
    it says nothing at all
        but just stands there
           with the patience

of vegetables
    and saints
        until the whole earth has turned around
           and the silver moon

becomes the golden sun—
    as the lily absolutely knew it would,
        which is itself, isn't it,
           the perfect prayer?

Look and See

This morning, at waterside, a sparrow flew
to a water rock and landed, by error, on the back
of an eider duck; lightly it fluttered off, amused.
The duck, too, was not provoked, but, you might say, was
laughing.

This afternoon a gull sailing over
our house was casually scratching
its stomach of white feathers with one
pink foot as it flew.

Oh Lord, how shining and festive is your gift to us, if we
only look, and see.

This World

I would like to write a poem about the world that has in it
nothing fancy.
But it seems impossible.
Whatever the subject, the morning sun
glimmers it.
The tulip feels the heat and flaps its petals open
and becomes a star.
The ants bore into the peony bud and there is the dark
  pinprick well of sweetness.
As for the stones on the beach, forget it.
Each onc could be set in gold.
So I tried with my eyes shut, but of course the birds
  were singing.
And the aspen trees were shaking the sweetest music
  out of their leaves.
And that was followed by, guess what, a momentous and
  beautiful silence
as comes to all of us, in little earfuls, if we're not too
  hurried to hear it.
As for spiders, how the dew hangs in their webs
  even if they say nothing, or seem to say nothing.
So fancy is the world, who knows, maybe they sing.
So fancy is the world, who know, maybe the stars sing too,
  and the ants, and the peonies, and the warm stones,
so happy to be where they are, on the beach, instead of being
  locked up in gold.

At Black River

All day
   its dark, slick bronze soaks
      in a mossy place,
         its teeth,

a multitude
   set
      for the comedy
         that never comes—

its tail
   knobbed and shiny,
      and with a heavy-weight's punch
         packed around the bone.

In beautiful Florida
   he is king
      of his own part
         of the black river,

and from his nap
   he will wake
      into the warm darkness
         to boom, and thrust forward,

paralyzing
   the swift, thin-waisted fish,
      or the bird
         in its frilled, white gown,

that has dipped down
   from the heaven of leaves
      one last time,
         to drink.

Don't think
   I'm not afraid.
      There is such an unleashing
         of horror.

Then I remember:
   death comes before
      the rolling away
         of the stone.

The Marsh Hawk

The marsh hawk
   doesn't,
      as other hawks do,
         work his wings

like soft hinges
   to make
      progress over
         the morning marsh,

but merely,
   or so it seems,
      lays his breast upon the air
         and the air, as if understanding,

floats him along
   with his wings open,
      and raised, just a little
         beyond the horizontal—in thanks, perhaps,

to the great crystal carrier
   of leaves and clouds—
      of everything.
         And even though his shadow

follows exactly
   his every tilt and flow, and even though
      he must know that hunger will win,
         he doesn't hurry,

but floats in wide circles
   as he gazes
      into the marshes below
         his hard beak

and the hooks of his feet, as though
   wanting something
      more lasting than meat.
         At noon he's still there

above the brambles, the grass, the flat water,
   where, in their almost stately disengagement,
      the inedible dampness and darkness
         shine.

Breakage

I go down to the edge of the sea.
How everything shines in the morning light!
The cusp of the whelk,
the broken cupboard of the clam,
the opened, blue mussels,
moon snails, pale pink and barnacle scarred—
and nothing at all whole or shut, but tattered, split,
dropped by the gulls onto the gray rocks and all the
   moisture gone.
It's like a schoolhouse
of little words,
thousands of words.
First you figure out what each one means by itself,
the jingle, the periwinkle, the scallop
   full of moonlight.

Then you begin, slowly, to read the whole story.

Where Does the Dance Begin,
Where Does It End?

Don't call this world adorable, or useful, that's not it.
It's frisky, and a theater for more than fair winds.
The eyelash of lightning is neither good nor evil.
The struck tree burns like a pillar of gold.

But the blue rain sinks, straight to the white
   feet of the trees
whose mouths open.
Doesn't the wind, turning in circles, invent the dance?
Haven't the flowers moved, slowly, across Asia, then Europe,
   until at last, now, they shine
     in your own yard?

Don't call this world an explanation, or even an education.

When the Sufi poet whirled, was he looking
outward, to the mountains so solidly there
in a white-capped ring, or was he looking

to the center of everything: the seed, the egg, the idea
that was also there,
beautiful as a thumb
curved and touching the finger, tenderly,
little love-ring,

as he whirled,
oh jug of breath,
in the garden of dust?

Snow Geese

Oh, to love what is lovely, and will not last!
   What a task
      to ask

of anything, or anyone,

yet it is ours,
   and not by the century or the year, but by the hours.

One fall day I heard
   above me, and above the sting of the wind, a sound
I did not know, and my look shot upward; it was

a flock of snow geese, winging it
   faster than the ones we usually see,
and, being the color of snow, catching the sun

so they were, in part at least, golden. I

held my breath
as we do
sometimes
to stop time
when something wonderful
has touched us

as with a match
which is lit, and bright,
but does not hurt
in the common way,

but delightfully,
as if delight
were the most serious thing
you ever felt.

The geese
flew on.
I have never
seen them again.

Maybe I will, someday, somewhere.
Maybe I won't.
It doesn't matter.
What matters
is that, when I saw them,
I saw them
as through the veil, secretly, joyfully, clearly.

What Was Once the Largest Shopping Center in Northern Ohio Was Built Where There Had Been a Pond I Used to Visit Every Summer Afternoon

Loving the earth, seeing what has been done to it,
I grow sharp, I grow cold.

Where will the trilliums go, and the coltsfoot?
Where will the pond lilies go to continue living
their simple, penniless lives, lifting
their faces of gold?

Impossible to believe we need so much
as the world wants us to buy.
I have more clothes, lamps, dishes, paper clips
than I could possibly use before I die.

Oh, I would like to live in an empty house,
with vines for walls, and a carpet of grass.
No planks, no plastic, no fiberglass.

And I suppose sometime I will.
Old and cold I will lie apart
from all this buying and selling, with only
the beautiful earth in my heart.

The Dovekie

Whatever
you know
about *here*
it doesn't

tell you
anything
about
what happens

out there.
The dovekie,
for example,
is smaller

than the robin
who eats the cherries
in the tree
in your yard

and the worms
in your grass.
It is white and black.
It lays

a single egg
in cold country
in the brief summer;
its wings

buzz as it flies
over the waters.
Listen,
once again,

as again, and again,
we are given
this single wisdom:
to know

our world
is to be busy
all day long
with happiness.

If you are not
among us
I say
take boat;

go north;
row and stare
until you see him,
smaller than a robin,

in the burning cold,
in the black and white waters
singing his wren song
to the hungry waves.

Something

Something fashioned
this yellow-white lace-mass
that the sea has brought to the shore
and left —

like popcorn stuck to itself,
or a string of lace rolled up tight,
or a handful of fingerling shells pasted together,
each with a tear where something

escaped into the sea. I brought it home
out of the uncombed morning and consulted
among my books. I do not know
what to call this sharpest desire

to discover a name,
but there it is, suddenly, clearly
illustrated on the page, offering my heart
another singular

moment of happiness: to know that it is
the egg case of an ocean shell,
the whelk,
which, in its proper season,

spews forth its progeny in such
glutenous and faintly
glimmering fashion, each one
chewing and tearing itself free

while what is left rides to shore, one more
sweet-as-honey answer for the wanderer
whose tongue is agile, whose mind,
in the world's riotous plenty,

wants syntax, connections, lists,
and most of all names to set beside the multitudinous
stars, flowers, sea creatures, rocks, trees.
The egg case of the whelk

sits on my shelf in front of, as it happens, Blake.
Sometimes I dream
that everything in the world is here, in my room,
in a great closet, named and orderly,

and I am here too, in front of it,
hardly able to see for the flash and the brightness—
and sometimes I am that madcap person clapping my hands and singing;
and sometimes I am that quiet person down on my knees.

Logos

Why wonder about the loaves and the fishes?
If you say the right words, the wine expands.
If you say them with love
and the felt ferocity of that love
and the felt necessity of that love,
the fish explode into many.
Imagine him, speaking,
and don't worry about what is reality,
or what is plain, or what is mysterious.
If you were there, it was all those things.
If you can imagine it, it is all those things.
Eat, drink, be happy.
Accept the miracle.
Accept, too, each spoken word
spoken with love.

Bear

It's not my track,
I say, seeing
the ball of the foot and the wide heel
and the naily, untrimmed
toes. And I say again,
for emphasis,

to no one but myself, since no one is
with me. This is
not my track, and this is an extremely
large foot, I wonder
how large a body must be to make
such a track, I am beginning to make

bad jokes. I have read probably
a hundred narratives where someone saw
just what I am seeing. Various things
happened next. A fairly long list, I won't

go into it. But not one of them told
what happened next—I mean, before whatever happens—

how the distances light up, how the clouds
are the most lovely shapes you have ever seen, how

the wild flowers at your feet begin distilling a fragrance
different, and sweeter than any you ever stood upon before—how

every leaf on the whole mountain is aflutter.

Many Miles

The feet of the heron,
under those bamboo stems,
hold the blue body,
the great beak

above the shallows
of the pond.
Who could guess
their patience?

Sometimes the toes
shake, like worms.
What fish
could resist?

Or think of the cricket,
his green hooks
climbing the blade of grass—
or think of camel feet

like ear muffs,
striding over the sand—
or think of your own
slapping along the highway,

a long life,
many miles.
To each of us comes
the body gift.

Luna

In the early curtains
  of the dusk
    it flew,
      a slow galloping

this way and that way
  through the trees
    and under the trees.
      I live

in the open mindedness
  of not knowing enough
    about anything.
      It was beautiful.

It was silent.
  It didn't even have a mouth.
    But it wanted something,
      it had a purpose

and a few precious hours
  to find it,
    and I suppose it did.
      The next evening

it lay on the ground
  like a broken leaf
    and didn't move,
      which hurt my heart

which is another small thing
   that doesn't know much.
      When this happened it was about
         the middle of summer,

which also has its purposes
   and only so many precious hours.
      How quietly,
         and not with any assignment from us,

or even a small hint
   of understanding,
      everything that needs to be done
         is done.

"Just a minute," said a voice . . .

"Just a minute," said a voice in the weeds.
So I stood still
in the day's exquisite early morning light
and so I didn't crush with my great feet
any small or unusual thing just happening to pass by
where I was passing by
on my way to the blueberry fields,
and maybe it was the toad
and maybe it was the June beetle
and maybe it was the pink and tender worm
who does his work without limbs or eyes
and does it well
or maybe it was the walking stick, still frail
and walking humbly by, looking for a tree,
or maybe, like Blake's wondrous meeting, it was
the elves, carrying one of their own
on a rose-petal coffin away, away
into the deep grasses. After awhile
the quaintest voice said, "Thank you." And then there was silence.
For the rest, I would keep you wondering.

PART
TWO

This Morning I Watched the Deer

This morning I watched the deer
   with beautiful lips touching the tips
of the cranberries, setting their hooves down
   in the dampness carelessly, isn't it after all
the carpet of their house, their home, whose roof
   is the sky?

Why, then, was I suddenly miserable?

Well, this is nothing much.
This is the heaviness of the body watching the swallows
   gliding just under that roof.

This is the wish that the deer would not lift their heads
   and leap away, leaving me there alone.
This is the wish to touch their faces, their brown wrists—
   to sing some sparkling poem into
the folds of their ears,

then walk with them,
over the hills
and over the hills

and into the impossible trees.

The Old Poets of China

Wherever I am, the world comes after me.
It offers me its busyness. It does not believe
that I do not want it. Now I understand
why the old poets of China went so far and high
into the mountains, then crept into the pale mist.

White-eyes

In winter
all the singing is in
the tops of the trees
where the wind-bird

with its white eyes
shoves and pushes
among the branches.
Like any of us

he wants to go to sleep,
but he's restless—
he has an idea,
and slowly it unfolds

from under his beating wings
as long as he stays awake.
But his big, round music, after all,
is too breathy to last.

So, it's over.
In the pine-crown
he makes his nest,
he's done all he can.

I don't know the name of this bird,
I only imagine his glittering beak
tucked in a white wing
while the clouds—

which he has summoned
    from the north—
        which he has taught
            to be mild, and silent—

thicken, and begin to fall
    into the world below
        like stars, or the feathers
            of some unimaginable bird

that loves us,
    that is asleep now, and silent—
        that has turned itself
        into snow.

Yellowlegs

With three sharp cries, each one the shape of a rainbow,
  yellowlegs comes on fast wings to the place of the little waves
and the little fish. It has

dapples too many to count, and a long neck, and a
  bright eye, and knees like yellow rose buds just beginning
to open. The water is blue

or transparent. The fish
  are almost invisible but their dark shadows fly
just above the sand at the bottom
  of the cold water. They too are too many to count—

so many plus two or three that have vanished already
  into yellowlegs' long, slightly curved twig of a beak.
Two or three, enough to satisfy the appetite—all the
  difference between
nothing and everything, all this: this ocean, this world.

The Best I Could Do

In the black-shadowed pines
on the shore
beyond the pond
owl was sitting.
When he saw me
his eyes flared like matches
and he did his big, loose hunch,
stirring up the bronze of his shoulders,

and hissed,
and seemed about to fly away.
Who knows why he didn't but instead
clamped his orange feet down
on the black limb
and stared into my face, though not my eyes—
had I been mouse or squirrel
I would have cried

for my life. And thus we stayed
for a long time. I would have given
a great deal
to have invoked some connection,
eye to eye,
to know what he thought of me

here in the world—*his* world—
his gauzy and furzy acres,
sour, weedy, lush,
mortal.
But except for the hiss, he did not make
the least sound, simply stared

as though if he wanted to he could lift me
and carry me away—
one orange knife for each shoulder, and I,
aloft in the air, under his great wings, shouting
praise, praise, praise as I cried
for my life.

The Wren from Carolina

Just now the wren from Carolina buzzed
through the neighbor's hedge
a line of grace notes I couldn't even write down
much less sing.

Now he lifts his chestnut colored throat
and delivers such a cantering praise—
for what?
For the early morning, the taste of the spider,

for his small cup of life
that he drinks from every day, knowing it will refill.
All things are inventions of holiness.
Some more rascally than others.

I'm on that list too,
though I don't know exactly where.
But, every morning, there's my own cup of gladness,
and there's that wren in the hedge, above me, with his

blazing song.

Some Things, Say the Wise Ones

Some things, say the wise ones who know everything,
are not living. I say,
you live your life your way and leave me alone.

I have talked with the faint clouds in the sky whey they
are afraid of being left behind; I have said, Hurry, hurry!
and they have said: Thank you, we are hurrying.

About cows, and starfish, and roses, there is no
argument. They die, after all.

But water is a question, so many living things in it,
but what is it, itself, living or not? Oh, gleaming

generosity, how can they write you out?

As I think this I am sitting on the sand beside
the harbor. I am holding in my hand
small pieces of granite, pyrite, schist.
Each one, just now, so thoroughly asleep.

Mindful

Every day
 I see or I hear
  something
   that more or less

kills me
 with delight,
  that leaves me
   like a needle

in the haystack
 of light.
  It is what I was born for—
   to look, to listen,

to lose myself
 inside this soft world—
  to instruct myself
   over and over

in joy,
 and acclamation.
  Nor am I talking
   about the exceptional,

the fearful, the dreadful,
 the very extravagant—
  but of the ordinary,
   the common, the very drab,

the daily presentations.
   Oh, good scholar,
      I say to myself,
         how can you help

but grow wise
   with such teachings
      as these—
         the untrimmable light

of the world,
   the ocean's shine,
      the prayers that are made
        out of grass?

Song of the Builders

On a summer morning
I sat down
on a hillside
to think about God—

a worthy pastime.
Near me, I saw
a single cricket;
it was moving the grains of the hillside

this way and that way.
How great was its energy,
how humble its effort.
Let us hope

it will always be like this,
each of us going on
in our inexplicable ways
building the universe.

Look Again

What you have never noticed about the toad, probably,
is that his tongue is attached not to the back of his mouth but
the front—how far it extends
when the fly hesitates on a near-enough leaf! Or that

his front feet, which are sometimes padded, hold three nimble
digits—had anyone
a piano small enough I think the toad could learn
to play something, a little Mozart maybe, inside
the cool cellar of the sandy hill—and if

the eyes bulge they have gold rims,
and if the smile is wide it never fails,
and the warts, the delicate uplifts of dust-colored skin, are
neither random nor suggestive of dolor, but rather are
little streams of jewelry, in patterns of espousal and pleasure,
running up and down their crooked backs, sweet and alive in the sun.

Goldenrod, Late Fall

This morning the goldenrod are all wearing
    their golden shirts
fresh from heaven's soft wash in the chill night.
    So it must be a celebration.
And here comes the wind, so many swinging wings!
    Has he been invited, or is he the intruder?
Invited, whisper the golden pebbles of the weeds,
    as they begin to fall

over the ground. Well, you would think the little murmurs
    of the broken blossoms would have said
otherwise, but no. So I sit down among them to
    think about it while all around me the crumbling
goes on. The weeds let down their seedy faces
    cheerfully, which is the part I like best, and certainly

it is as good as a book for learning from. You would think
    they were just going for a small sleep. You would think
they couldn't wait, it was going to be
    that snug and even, as all their lives were, full of
excitation. You would think

it was a voyage just beginning, and no darkness anywhere,
    but tinged with all necessary instruction, and light,

and all were shriven, as all the round world is,
    and so it wasn't anything but easy to fall, to whisper
Good Night.

November

The snow
began slowly,
a soft and easy
sprinkling

of flakes, then clouds of flakes
in the baskets of the wind
and the branches
of the trees—

oh, so pretty.
We walked
through the growing stillness,
as the flakes

prickled the path,
then covered it,
then deepened
as in curds and drifts,

as the wind grew stronger,
shaping its work
less delicately,
taking greater steps

over the hills
and through the trees
until, finally,
we were cold,

and far from home.
We turned
and followed our long shadows back
to the house,

stamped our feet,
went inside, and shut the door.
Through the window
we could see

how far away it was to the gates of April.
Let the fire now
put on its red hat
and sing to us.

Daisies

It is possible, I suppose, that sometime
   we will learn everything
there is to learn: what the world is, for example,
   and what it means. I think this as I am crossing
from one field to another, in summer, and the
   mockingbird is mocking me, as one who either
knows enough already or knows enough to be
   perfectly content not knowing. Song being born
of quest he knows this: he must turn silent
   were he suddenly assaulted with answers. Instead

oh hear his wild, caustic, tender warbling ceaselessly
   unanswered. At my feet the white-petaled daisies display
the small suns of their center-piece—their, if you don't
   mind my saying so—their hearts. Of course
I could be wrong, perhaps their hearts are pale and
   narrow and hidden in the roots. What do I know.
But this: it is heaven itself to take what is given,
   to see what is plain; what the sun
lights up willingly; for example—I think this
   as I reach down, not to pick but merely to touch—
the suitability of the field for the daisies, and the
   daisies for the field.

One

The mosquito is so small
it takes almost nothing to ruin it.
Each leaf, the same.
And the black ant, hurrying.
So many lives, so many fortunes!
Every morning, I walk softly and with forward glances
down to the ponds and through the pinewoods.
Mushrooms, even, have but a brief hour
before the slug creeps to the feast,
before the pine needles hustle down
under the bundles of harsh, beneficent rain.

How many, how many, how many
make up a world!
And then I think of that old idea: the singular
  and the eternal.
One cup, in which everything is swirled
back to the color of the sea and the sky.
Imagine it!

A shining cup, surely!
In the moment in which there is no wind
over your shoulder,
you stare down into it,
and there you are,
your own darling face, your own eyes.
And then the wind, not thinking of you, just passes by,

touching the ant, the mosquito, the leaf,
and you know what else!
How blue is the sea, how blue is the sky,
how blue and tiny and redeemable everything is, even you,
even your eyes, even your imagination.

The Soul at Last

The Lord's terrifying kindness has come to me.

It was only a small silvery thing—say a piece of silver cloth, or a thousand spider webs woven together, or a small handful of aspen leaves, with their silver backs shimmering. And it came leaping out of the closed coffin; it flew into the air, it danced snappingly around the church rafters, it vanished through the ceiling.

I spoke there, briefly, of the loved one gone. I gazed at the people in the pews, some of them weeping. I knew I must, someday, write this down.

The Pinewoods

Just before dawn
    three deer
        came walking
            down the hill

as if the moment were nothing different
    from eternity—
        as lightly as that
            they nibbled

the leaves,
    they drank
        from the pond,
            their pretty mouths

sucking the loose silver,
    their heavy eyes
        shining.
            Listen,

I did not really see them.
    I came later, and saw their tracks
        on the empty sand.
            But I don't believe

only to the edge
    of what my eyes actually see
        in the kindness of the morning,
            do you?

And my life,
　　which is my body surely,
　　　　is also something more—
　　　　　　isn't yours?

I suppose the deer waited
　　to see the sun lift itself up,
　　　　filling the hills with light and shadows—
　　　　　　then they went leaping

back into the rough, uncharted pinewoods
　　where I have lived so much of my life,
　　　　where everything is so quick and uncertain,
　　　　　　so glancing, so improbable, so real.

Lingering in Happiness

After rain after many days without rain,
it stays cool, private and cleansed, under the trees,
and the dampness there, married now to gravity,
falls branch to branch, leaf to leaf, down to the ground

where it will disappear—but not, of course, vanish
except to our eyes. The roots of the oaks will have their share,
and the white threads of the grasses, and the cushion of moss;
a few drops, round as pearls, will enter the mole's tunnel;

and soon so many small stones, buried for a thousand years,
will feel themselves being touched.

My thanks to the editors of the following periodicals, in which some of the poems in this volume first appeared.

"White-eyes," "Breakage," "At Black River" — *Poetry*

"Trout Lilies," "Where Does the Temple Begin, Where Does It End?" — *The Southern Review*

"Song of the Builders" — *Wilderness*

"Bone" — *Cape Cod Voice*

"The Snow Cricket" — *DoubleTake*

"One" — *Image*

"Many Miles" — *Oprah Magazine*

"Something" — *Spiritus*

"The Arrowhead," "Look Again," "Have You Seen Blacksnake Swimming?" — *Onearth* (formerly *Amicus*)

"Lingering in Happiness" appeared originally in *The New Yorker*